colorblind
photography

Being colorblind gives an advantage when composing black & white photography... less confusion.

This special collection selected from thousands of captures. All images were framed in the camera and presented without edits, genuine as seen through the lens with unique process.

Original fine art and custom work available.

info@ BEACHNOISE.com

Joseph Fleming

JH FLEMING
© 2015 ALL RIGHTS RESERVED

0780

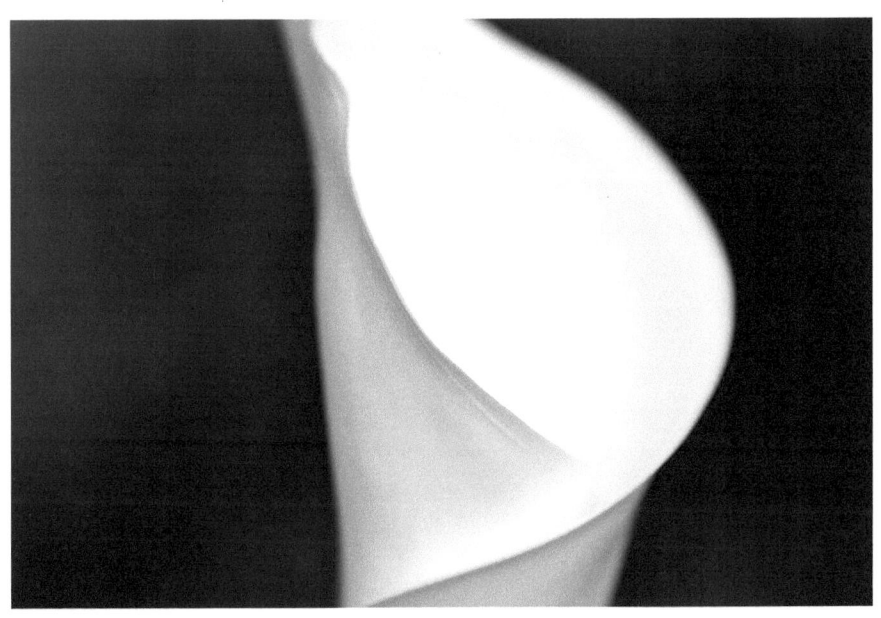

0920

1581

1608

2180

2467

2962

3151

3359

3937

4035

4070

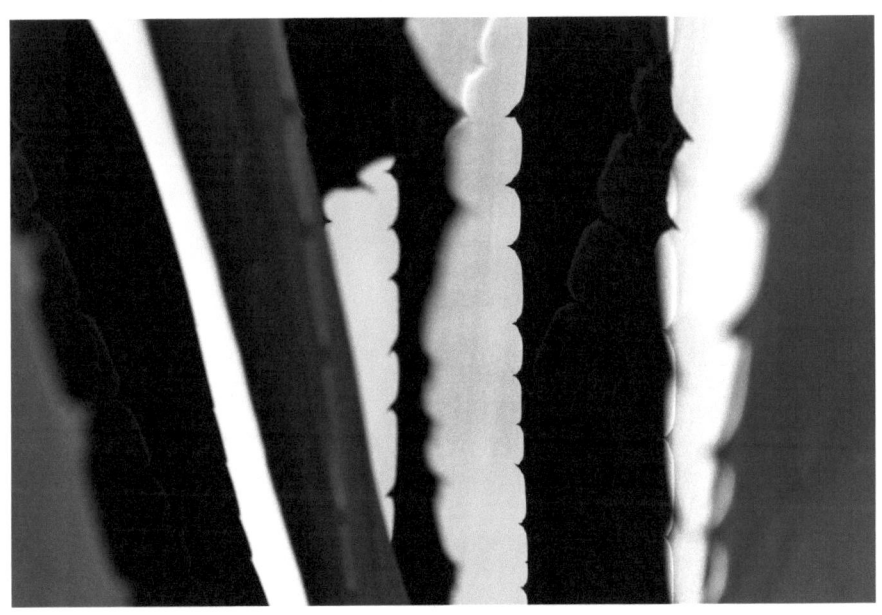

4099

5492

5750

5811

6095

7182

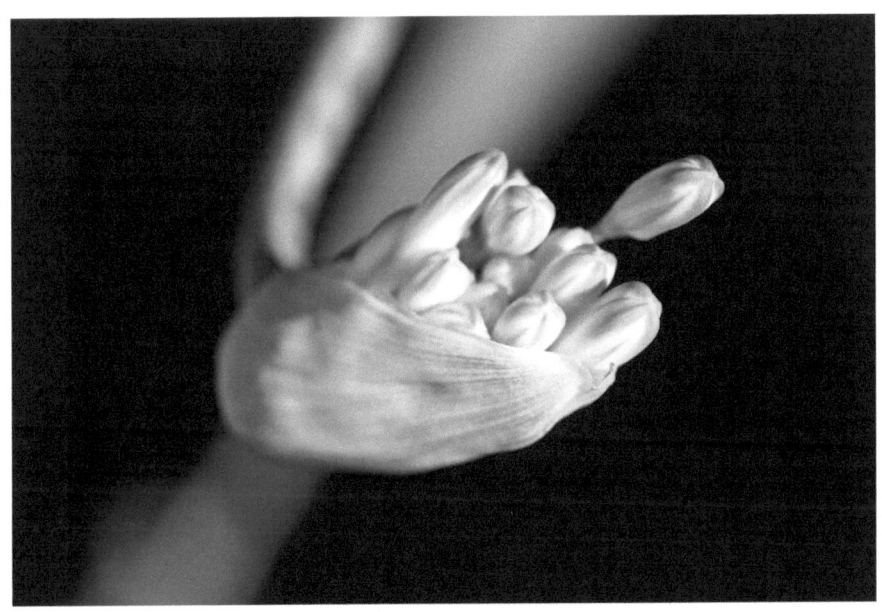

8407

8470

9024

9353

9430

www.ingramcontent.com/pod-product-compliance
Lightning Source LLC
Chambersburg PA
CBHW040919180526
45159CB00002BA/536